The Reflective Journal for Practitioners

Working in Abuse and Trauma

Created by

Dr Jessica Eaton

Book cover design by Johnson Marketing.

First Printing: October 2019

ISBN 978-0-244-19834-3

Dr Jessica Eaton T/A VictimFocus

Derbyshire, UK

www.victimfocus.org.uk

Email: Jessica@victimfocus.org.uk

Ordering Information:

Special discounts are available on quantity purchases by corporations, associations, educators, and others. For details, contact the publisher at the above listed address.

This journal is dedicated to the thousands of committed practitioners, volunteers and students who are working to support people subjected to violence, trauma and abuse.

Contents

How to use this reflective journal

A foreword by Dr Jessica Eaton

Welcome to your new reflective journal. You must be here because like me, you work in trauma, abuse or violence. You might work with children, adults or whole families. Statutory, voluntary or private sector – this journal is for you.

I designed this journal with all of us in mind. We are all doing jobs that will distress us, exhaust us and challenge us. Yet despite this reality, many of us are not provided with adequate psychological support, reflective supervision or critical perspectives to help us along the way.

Inside this journal is ten sections of reflection questions that are designed to help you think critically about your own values, practice, skills, knowledge, strategies and experiences.

You can use this journal however you like. There are over 230 pages of reflective tasks which include sentence completion, doodling, lists, questions and anecdotes. They are split into sections and each section begins with an explanation of the types of tasks that are included.

You may wish to use this journal once per day or once per week. It could be that you flick through the journal until you find a task that really jumps out at you or resonates with how you are feeling that day. Alternatively, you might decide to work methodically through this journal and complete one task per day until completed. You could also read the contents page and then choose which section you want to complete. The choice is yours and this journal is private, confidential and personal to you.

You can shout, swear, challenge yourself, challenge the system, cry, celebrate and big yourself up in this journal. You can read a question and come back to it another day. You can choose to answer 10 questions in a day if you need to reflect on something that is bothering you.

This journal is not designed to replace reflective or clinical supervision. My view is that we are all entitled to that support when working in trauma, violence and abuse. However, I do acknowledge the reality – that most of us are not getting the support, self-care and supervision we need.

The journal contains contentious, difficult, challenging, critical and interesting questions. It is for those who are ready to question themselves, to question the system and to question whether we are doing the best we can do for ourselves and for our clients. Like most reflective tasks, you will get out of it what you put into it. If you choose not to dig deep or to be honest with yourself whilst answering the questions, you will only ever scratch the surface of the critical reflection you are truly capable of. However, if you are willing to use this journal as your personal space for self-reflection, learning and development – you are certain to gain a lot from using this journal.

I hope you enjoy using this journal and they become part of your self-care routine for many years to come.

Thank you for everything you are doing in our field of trauma, abuse and violence. You will never know how many lives you have touched.

Thank you for committing to self-reflection and self-development.

SECTION 1

STRENGTHS BASED PRACTICE AND TRAUMA INFORMED REFLECTIONS

A section containing questions about strengths, talents, skills and experiences of your clients. These questions and tasks are mixed in with trauma-informed, anti-stigma tasks that challenge the medical model of mental health.

Use this section to help you to see the strengths of your client or your work and to challenge the medicalisation and labelling of your client.

1. Describe your client using only their strengths

2. Think about the client you are most worried about. Picture them happy, healthy and looking forward to their future. Write about what you see.

3. Write about what triggers your client and what their triggers mean to them

4. If you only looked at the strengths and skills of the clients in your most difficult case, how would it change the way you described them?

5. Write about all the things that make your client happy

6. Doodle your client surrounded by the things that make them feel safe

7. Think about how your client acts, thinks and feels when they are traumatised. How can you help them when they feel like this?

8. Write about an ideal career or role for your client. What would they excel at and why?

9. Write about a client who has been given an incorrect psychiatric diagnosis instead of professionals recognising the trauma they were subjected to

10. I was so impressed when my client overcame...

11. Write about your client with no reference to disorders, medical language or psychiatric terms

12. Doodle your client in their happy place

13. If people could understand the trauma your client has lived through, what would change for them?

14. Write about a client who amazed you with their bravery

15. Doodle your client when they are feeling vulnerable. Now doodle them again when they are feeling strong and capable.

16. How do your client's coping mechanisms relate to their traumas?

17. Which traumas have impacted your client the most and how can you help them?

18. What would you like to teach your client about trauma?

19. If you could tell your client about their strengths and talents, what would you tell them?

20. Write about a life lesson or a piece of wisdom you learned from a client

21. Think about a coping mechanism your client has. How did it develop and how does it protect them?

22. Doodle your relationship with your client at the moment

23. What is your client good at and how can you encourage them?

24. Write about a client who always made you laugh

25. Write the questions you would like to ask your client in order to learn more about how you can help them process their trauma

26. I have a client who is capable of great things, but they cannot see it yet. I am going to help them to see it by…

27. How have some professionals misinterpreted the trauma of your client?

28. Write about a time when you have not understood someone's coping mechanisms or trauma responses

29. Write about a time when you helped a client to see their strengths or talents

30. One of the most inspirational clients I ever met was…

SECTION 2

CASE PROGRESSION AND UNDERSTANDING YOUR CLIENT

This section contains tasks that can help you to explore the progress you and your client is making. It also contains tasks and questions to explore whether you understand the experiences of your client.

Use this section when you want to understand your client better or when you feel that there is something you are missing or misunderstanding. You can also use this section to explore why progress might have slowed or stopped.

1. What has been going well for your client recently?

2. I wish I understood my client more when they talk about...

3. What have you done to earn the respect of your client?

4. Tomorrow, your client wins £1000 in a competition, what do they spend it on?

5. If your client was the main character in a film about their life, how would their film end? Write three alternative endings.

6. Think about your most challenging case. Write about the qualities you love about the client in that case

7. Doodle your client surrounded by the barriers and hurdles they need to overcome to make the progress they want to make

8. Think about the behaviours of your client. How does the outside world perceive those behaviours? What do those behaviours really mean?

9. What external factors are stopping your client from reaching their full potential?

10. Write about a case you didn't handle as well as you would have liked to

11. Write a letter to your client who feels stuck in a situation

12. One thing I would love to say to my client is…

13. If I had control over the services I provided to my client, I would make sure they had access to…

14. One year from now, your client reports feeling happy, safe and confident. What would need to change for this to happen?

15. Write about the barriers to success for your client and how you can help to break those barriers down

16. Think about a time when you misunderstood a client. Why did that happen?

17. Reflect on how far your client has already come

18. Which services are blocking the progress of your client and what can you do about it?

19. Doodle your client leaping over the hurdles in their lives

20. Where do you see your client in 12 months' time?

21. Why is progress so slow with your client at the moment? What do you think needs to change?

22. I'm so proud of my client for the immense progress they have made with…

23. If I could ask my client one personal question, I would ask them…

24. How can I make sure that my client feels like they are making steps towards their goals?

25. Write about a time when you felt like there was no way you could help your client to move forward

SECTION 3

REFLECTING ON OPPRESSION AND DISCRIMINATION

This section contains tasks and questions that will help you to focus on the ways that oppression, discrimination and 'isms' are affecting your work and your clients. It is a challenging section but is important for us all to remain aware of the ways privilege, power, institutional discrimination and oppressive practice change our decisions and thought processes.

Use this section when you want to explore the way oppression, discrimination, power and privilege are affecting your practice or your client.

1. How does oppression play a role in your line of work?

2. Write about an example of practice that was oppressive or harmful towards a client

3. I believe unconscious bias is...

4. Doodle what would need to change to eliminate inequality
   in society

5. Do you think all your clients are seen equally by all services and professionals? Why/why not?

6. Write about the role of racism in your line of work

7. Which services in your area do you trust not to discriminate against clients?

8. Write about a time when your own beliefs or values led you to make assumptions about a client

9. Which group of clients are the most overlooked in your line
    of work?

10. Here are 3 ways sexism is impacting my client…

11. How do you challenge oppressive practice in your role?

12. Write about the role of homophobia in your line of work

13. Doodle all the oppressions, inequalities and injustices you have seen in your line of work. Now doodle a huge hammer smashing them to pieces.

14. Have you been subjected to oppression in your own life? How does your experience (or lack of experience) change the way you work?

15. Classism is rarely talked about but affects many people.
Why do you think this is?

16. Think about the way different oppressions intersect. How is this affecting your client?

17. Write about the last time one of your clients suffered an injustice

18. Consider your own privileges and experiences. How do they change the way you think?

19. Write about a time when you had to face someone else's sense of entitlement

20. Here are 3 ways racism is impacting my client...

21. If I heard a colleague discriminate against someone, I would say/do...

22. Write about beliefs you used to hold about groups of people until they were challenged or changed

23. I think ageism is...

24. How did your upbringing change the way you understood oppression and privilege?

25. How are power structures impacting your client?

26. Write about the role of sexism in your line of work

27. Here are 3 way that classism changes the way we work with our clients…

28. Write about personal views you hold that you are not comfortable sharing with others and why you feel that discomfort

29. 'All people are equal these days' – Write your response to this statement

30. Doodle your client feeling powerful and respected in the world

SECTION 4

REFLECTING ON BARRIERS AND FRUSTRATION

This section contains tasks and questions about barriers, problems and frustration at work. It might be that you feel something is blocking your progress, or that there are barriers to your client getting the best service or support.

Use this section when you want to process why you are feeling stuck, or why your client keeps coming up against barriers and blockages.

1. Doodle yourself surrounded by everything that is
frustrating you at the moment

2. Write about a recent decision that you felt was unfair

3. Your frustration could be positive – list 3 ways your frustration could be used effectively

4. What are your best strategies for when you feel the
   system is working against you?

5. What is stopping you from doing your best work at the moment?

6. Doodle yourself sitting in an empty room. On the walls, graffiti all your frustrations and barriers to success.

7. Write about a decision that you would like to see overturned

8. How are you going to influence that person who is blocking your progress?

9. Plan how you are going to overcome the barrier that is holding you back at the moment

10. I am frustrated because...

11. What did you do the last time you felt this stuck with a problem?

12. Write about a client who has overcome their own barriers recently

13. Doodle your client smashing all their own barriers

14. What or who is stopping you from reaching your full
    potential? How will you overcome this?

15. What did you do the last time you felt a client was not getting the service they deserved or needed?

16. Rage at the system. Go on. Let it all out. No one will see.

17. Write about a time when your anger or frustration caused you to make a positive change

18. How do you feel about working within the confines of the system you're in?

19. I recently came up against this barrier and this is how it made me feel…

20. Who do you draw your strength from when you feel powerless?

21. Why do people put barriers in the way of our success or progress?

22. What internal barriers are you coming up against?

23. Do you believe in the 'self-fulfilling prophecy'?

24. List all the negative ways you cope with your anger and frustration and then list all the positive ways you cope with it. Ponder your lists.

25. Write about a time when you supported a colleague who was feeling stuck or frustrated with a case

SECTION 5

REFLECTING ON YOUR OWN BELIEFS

This section contains personal questions about your own beliefs and values that might change the way you think or practice. Answer them honestly or take some time to think about them.

Use this section to learn more about yourself and how your own beliefs change the way you see the world.

1. 'Everyone holds biases, but not everyone admits them'. Jot down your thoughts about this statement

2. Do you believe that the criminal justice system is effective? Why/why not?

3. What beliefs were you brought up with that you later rejected? Why did you reject them?

4. Write about a time when someone accused you of holding offensive or biased beliefs.

5. Do you believe that people generally get what they deserve in life? How does this relate to your clients and their traumas?

6. Write about a time when your personal beliefs were challenged at work

7. Do you believe in the death penalty? Why/why not?

8. How do biases affect the type of work you do?

9. Do you have any beliefs that you have to 'leave at the door' when you go to work? Why do you leave them at the door?

10. Write about the last time you challenged someone else's beliefs

11. Do you believe the world is a fair place to live? How does this relate to your line of work?

12. How does having (or not having) a faith change the way you work with your clients?

13. How would you know if you held beliefs that were affecting your work?

14. Who do you go to when you need to 'sense check' your beliefs or thoughts about an issue?

15. How do your political beliefs change the way you work?

16. Are there any groups of people you feel nervous or uncomfortable working with? Why do you think that is?

17. Write about a belief you used to hold, that you now
discourage others from holding

18. How has this line of work changed your beliefs?

19. Do you hold any beliefs that you do not feel able to talk about in public or in the workplace? What are they and why can't you talk about them freely?

20. Write about a belief that you hold that makes other people feel uncomfortable

21. Do you believe that the world is generally good with a few bad apples, or that the world is a bad barrel with a few good apples?

22. How do you feel about people who hold offensive views or beliefs? Do they have a right to freedom of speech and beliefs, even if those beliefs offend others?

23. Write about a belief that is generally held by your
    organisation, but that you do not personally agree with

24. Unpopular opinions. We all have them. What is yours?

25. Do you believe in upward social mobility? That anyone can become anything if they just work harder?

26. Write about the last time you were forced to re-evaluate something you believed

SECTION 6

SELF CARE AND PERSONAL EXPERIENCES

This section is about your own psychological wellbeing. It is another very personal section with some challenging questions. It explores your own experiences, childhood, triggers and stressors.

Use this section when you want to explore how you are coping and processing the traumas in your own life and workplace.

1. Write about the first case that changed the way you looked at the world

2. Is it really possible to 'leave your own stuff at the door' and to be completely objective at work?

3. Do you get enough psychological support in your line of work?

4. Draw a grid across this page to make four boxes. In each box, doodle a 'part' of your identity or who you are.

5. How do you like to debrief after a stressful day?

6. How did your life experiences influence your career direction?

7. Would you prefer to have all the knowledge of the world that you have now, and be aware – or have none of that knowledge and be oblivious?

8. How effective are your own coping mechanisms?

9. Have you ever been worried about admitting your own traumas or experiences at work?

10. How do you and your colleagues support each other when things get tough?

11. How have you changed since starting this line of work?

12. Are we really role models to our clients if we cannot admit our own traumas, fears and experiences?

13. Write about a case you can't stop worrying about. Get it all out. List all your worries here.

14. Doodle yourself doing an easier job. You know. The job you always threaten to go and get when you are having a bad day.

15. Do you think there will come a time when you cannot do this work anymore?

16. List some ideas for your own self-care after a stressful day

17. Write about a case that triggered you back to your own traumas or experiences

18. My childhood influences the way I work because...

19. Write about a time when you coped well with a distressing case

20. Doodle your most common coping mechanisms. Your real ones. Not the ones you tell your supervisor about.

21. What skills and values have your own life experiences
given to you? How do you use them at work?

22. How do you try to protect those around you from the impact of your work?

23. What would Little You think of Big You?

24. How has this line of work changed the way you see the criminal justice system?

25. Ignorance is bliss. Consider this statement in relation to your line of work and the people around you who remain oblivious to it.

26. What unique strengths and viewpoints do you bring to this work?

27. Doodle yourself being totally proud of who you are, what you have lived through and where you come from

28. Do you ever worry that you are getting desensitized to things that should horrify you?

SECTION 7

MIRACLE QUESTIONS AND FINDING SOLUTIONS

This section contains questions and thinking tasks that encourage you to find solutions by using hypothetical miracle situations. When used carefully, we can use miracle questions to get to the bottom of our problems, by focusing us on what needs to change.

Use this section when you want to think in a more solution-focussed way.

1. You bump into your client in 10 years' time and they are healthy, happy and successful. What changed for them?

2. Next month, you are offered a senior role in which you can create huge systemic change. What do you do first and why?

3. One morning, you wake up and all your stress and frustrations about work have disappeared. What must have changed for you to feel like this?

4. The next time you see your client, they feel in control of their life and they are ready to make big changes. What changed to make this happen?

5. You are offered a £1 million to set up your own charitable
project. What project do you set up and how would it
work?

6. You walk into work and you are greeted exactly how you feel you should be. What is said to you and who by?

7. Your client calls you to say that they escaped the abuser and will never go back. What must have changed for them to have done this?

8. You wake up tomorrow morning and a miracle has happened overnight. The problem you are worried about has been solved, and your life has improved dramatically. Spend some time imagining this. What is the first thing you notice?

9. You are given the power to redesign the support that is given to your clients. What is the first thing you remove or ban?

10. Next week, your service announces a new budget to pay for any therapy, service provision or items that your clients need. What would be the first thing you applied for?

11. You meet your client and they tell you that the new therapy they have had has completely changed the way they are thinking about the issue. What changed and why?

12. You wake up tomorrow and you feel confident and capable and back in control. What must have changed overnight for you to feel this way?

SECTION 8

REFLECTING ON KNOWLEDGE, SKILLS AND RESOURCES

This section provides space for you to explore your own knowledge, skills, resources and gaps. It contains questions and sentence completion about what you already know, what you feel you need to know more about and what resources you need.

Use this section when you feel you need to review your own knowledge and skills.

1. What is your area of expertise and how did you gain that expertise?

2. Write about an area of knowledge you want to learn more about

3. My favourite topic to learn about is…

4. What skills do you have that you don't get to use in your current role?

5. Do you feel all your knowledge and skills are being applied in your current role?

6. What knowledge do you feel you need but do not currently have?

7. Which parts of your job do you feel that you are not trained well enough for?

8. Write your training wish list. What training courses would you love to attend?

9. One thing I feel I need to learn more about is...

10. Write about a case that made you feel out of your depth.
    What training or learning would have helped you?

11. Write your resource wish list. Which resources do you want or need? Why?

12. The best resource you have is yourself. Use this page to write about why you are your best resource for your clients.

13. I wish I had better skills in…

14. Write your book wish list. What books do you want to read
and why?

15. My favourite theory in my line of work is...

16. I learn best when I can…

17. What was the best training you ever attended and why?

18. If you could design a curriculum for everyone who does your job, what topics would you make mandatory?

19. What training is missing from your industry? Why is it missing?

20. How easily do you admit when you don't know how to do something?

21. You get given a £300 budget to spend on training or resources, what do you buy and why?

22. We are at our most dangerous when we assume that we know all there is to know. Discuss this perspective.

23. What was the worst training you had ever been on and why?

SECTION 9

REFLECTING ON PRACTICE SKILLS AND APPROACHES

This section contains questions, tasks and sentence completion to help you to explore your own practice skills, approaches and techniques. For some questions, you may find you do not know the answer and need to look it up. This is positive and supports your own reflective learning.

Use this section when you want to think about how to improve your own skills and knowledge.

1. How would you support someone who was blaming themselves for being abused?

2. Write 5 things you want to say to people who hate their body image after abuse

3. How do you help someone to ground out of a panic attack? List some of your techniques.

4. Write an explanation of coping mechanisms suitable for a 10-year-old

5. How would you describe love to a teenager?

6. What do you say when a client tells you they want to kill themselves?

7. How do you support a child who is not ready to disclose what is happening to them?

8. How would you work with parents who are blaming their child for being exploited?

9. Write a simple but accurate explanation of flashbacks

10. Discuss forgiveness. Is forgiveness really required for your client to move on and process their trauma?

11. How do you help someone who believes that their abuse is normal?

12. Write about the romanticisation of abuse and violence

13. What would you say to a colleague who was blaming children for being abused because they 'didn't protect themselves'?

14. If my client felt that our service was being sexist, I would say...

15. How do you help a pregnant teenage girl who doesn't know if she wants to keep her baby?

16. Write about a coping mechanism that is often misinterpreted by others as something else

17. How would you escalate a case that you felt was being overlooked or poorly assessed?

18. What would you do if you felt you were being manipulated
by carers of a child?

19. Explain sexuality in a way that would be suitable for an 8-year-old child who has been told at school that his big sister is a lesbian

20. How do you support someone who believes that their life will never get better?

21. How do you talk to someone about their self-harming?

22. How do you talk about mental health to your client without stigmatising and medicalising language?

23. If my client felt that our service was racist, I would...

24. How do you encourage parents to talk to their children about sex and relationships?

25. How do you work with someone who tells you that their suffering, trauma or oppression is a punishment from God for bad things they have done in their life?

26. What would you say to a child you are working with who is watching a lot of porn?

SECTION 10

SCRIBBLES, DOODLES AND DISTRACTIONS

This final section contains some fun and thought-provoking tasks to debrief, to distract yourself or to get some frustration out on to the page.

Use them whenever you need them.

SCRIBBLE YOUR RAGE PAGE #1

SCRIBBLE YOUR RAGE PAGE #2

SCRIBBLE YOUR RAGE PAGE #3

Write your favourite swear or curse word over and over again on
this page until you feel better or need a coffee

Doodle all the things in life that you are grateful for

Write your world laws. You know. For when you take over the world.

Doodle all of your favourite foods and drinks. Then go and find one of them and enjoy it.

Draw an outline of your face and write your emotions all over your own face. Not your real face. The drawing.

Draw yourself as a powerful superhero who can take on anything the world is going to throw at you.

Write the word GRUMPY over and over again in all different styles and fonts and colours until you are no longer grumpy.

Write all of the oppressions and injustices you hate most. Draw them at the bottom of the ocean, where they can stay forever.

Draw the person who inspires you to be better

Write a letter to your child-self. Tell them all the things that you wish others had told you.

Draw yourself at work. With a huge cup of coffee. The cup has to be bigger than your head.

Write about that favourite pen you once had before someone stole it and you never saw it again. Where did that go?

From memory, try to draw your computer or laptop keyboard with all the right keys in all the right places. Can you do it?

Draw yourself in 10 years' time. Who are you? Where are you? What are you doing? What are you wearing? Who are you with?

Eek! You finished your journal!

How do you feel?

What to do now:

- Read back through your journal and consider if any of your answers have changed over the months

- Consider which questions you didn't answer or struggled to answer

- Look at your doodles and feel proud of your creative genius

- Consider whether you want to keep this journal full of your ideas, thoughts and feelings… or kill it with fire

- Buy another one for next year

- Tell loads of people that they need a copy of this journal

- Wonder whether you should take that nice, normal job you have been dreaming of for years

- Keep on keeping on

- Carry on being reflective, critical and ready to learn

- Continue to change the world, one person at a time

- Pour a gin, mate